CONTENTS

Unusual Animal Facts

1   The only bird that can fly backward is the hummingbird.

2   The giant squid has the largest eyes in the world.

There's always one stray hummingbird in the flock who's got to show he can fly backward.

HHMMM
HMMM
HMMMM
HMMM

I won't fit in here for much longer at the rate they're feeding me!

3   Goldfish can grow up to 23 inches (58 cm) long and weigh over 6 pounds (2.7 kg).

4   A rat can survive longer without water than a camel.

5 **T**oupees for dogs are sold in Tokyo.

6 **A** dolphin sleeps with one eye open.

7 **A** crocodile cannot stick its tongue out.

8 **A** mammal's blood is red, an insect's blood is yellow, and a lobster's blood is blue.

9 **L**oud, fast music makes termites chew faster.

10 **A** blue whale's tongue weighs more than an elephant.

11 **A**n ostrich's eye is bigger than its brain.

12 **B**ats always exit a cave to the left.

13 **D**omestic cats kill an estimated one billion wild birds each year in the USA.

The scene at the entrance to the batcave at rush hour.

14 **T**igers have striped skin, not just striped fur.

Terry had to be careful in change rooms. For he had a secret. He was different from all the other tigers at school. Where they had stripes on their skin, ...Terry had spots!

15 **T**he blue whale's whistle is the loudest noise made by an animal.

16 **T**he heart of a giraffe weighs more than 25 lb (11 kg), is 2 ft (60 cm) wide, and has walls 3 in (7.5 cm) thick.

17 **C**amels have three eyelids to protect their eyes from blown sand.

18 **A** mole can dig a tunnel over 300 ft (90 m) long in just one night.

Even though a blind mole can dig a tunnel up to 300 feet long... that doesn't mean it knows where it's digging to.'

19 **E**lephants are not afraid of mice.

Elephants are not afraid of mice, but are very afraid of the similar looking Rogue Rwandan Rockhopping Rodent.

HI JUMBO!

20 **S**lugs have four noses.

21 **I**t is estimated that 25 percent of cat owners blow-dry their pets.

22 **O**nly female mosquitoes bite.

23 **S**nakes are immune to their own venom.

Don't tell me! It must have been the wash... the trim... the conditioner... and the BLOW DRY. Am I right?

7

24 **D**inosaurs probably lived to between 80 and 300 years of age. Scientists worked this out by looking at the structure of their bones.

25 **T**he fastest bird is the peregrine falcon. It can fly faster than 190 miles (300 km) per hour.

26 **I**n the Caribbean, there are oysters that can climb trees.

27 **M**osquitoes are attracted to the color blue more than any other color.

28 **C**ats cannot taste sweet things.

29   **M**any species of reptiles have two penises.

30   **H**erons have been observed dropping insects on the water, then catching the fish that surface to eat the insects.

The not so smart Heron comes to the realization that if dropping insects on the water attracts teensy weensy fish...it may also attract older hungrier not so friendly relatives as well.

31   **W**hen a mother cormorant feels her offspring are ready to leave the nest, she makes sure this happens by destroying the nest completely.

32   **T**he largest egg is laid by the ostrich. An ostrich egg can be 8 in (20 cm) in length and 6 in (15 cm) in diameter.

Oh brother! An ostrich egg! How am I going to eat all of it?

33 The smallest egg is laid by the humming-bird. Its egg is less than 0.39 in (1 cm) in diameter.

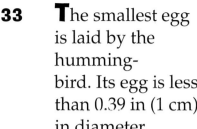

34 A blind chameleon is still able to change the color of its skin to match its environment.

Why you DON'T hear people saying... "At breakfast... I have my hummingbird egg... a piece of toast and jam and a cup of tea and I'm off to work for the day!"

OK..OK! Who's the wiseguy? I don't do that background!

35 Bald eagles can swim.

36 A zebra is white with black stripes, not black with white stripes.

37 The bird-eating spider from South America can have a legspan of 1 ft (30 cm).

Hey! Did you see that show on TV last night about those big black hairy bird eating spiders they have in South America?

I did! I'm sure glad we don't live there!

38 **S**tatistically you are more likely to be attacked by a cow than a shark.

39 **A**n eagle can kill and carry an animal as large as a small deer.

40 **A**t birth, a giant panda is smaller than a mouse.

41 **A** queen bee only uses her stinger to sting another queen bee.

42 **A**n elephant's gestation period can be up to 22 months.

43 **A** chameleon's tongue is twice the length of its body.

44 **T**o scare off enemies, the horned lizard squirts blood from its eyelids.

45 **S**pider silk, by weight, is stronger than steel.

46 **A** blue whale's heart only beats nine times per minute.

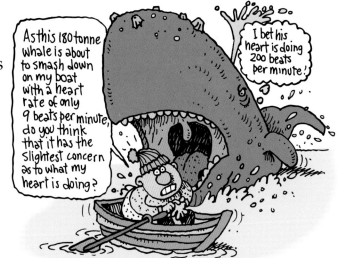

47 **A** hedgehog's heart beats 300 times per minute.

48 **H**orses can sleep standing up.

49 **A** cat needs four to five times more protein than a dog does.

50   **W**hen a baby kangaroo is born, it is about 0.8 in (2 cm) long.

51   **A**n electric eel can produce a shock of 600 volts. That's enough to knock a horse off its feet.

52   **C**himpanzees use tools more than any other animal, except humans.

The chimpanzees get some powertools for Christmas.

53   **L**obsters can regenerate their legs, claws, and antennae if these parts are pulled off by a predator.

54 **A** bald eagle's nest can be 12 ft (3.65 m) deep and 10 ft (3 m) wide.

55 **P**arrots live longer than any other type of bird. There are reliable reports of parrots living to 150 years of age.

56 **A**n African elephant has only four teeth.

57 **F**lying fish actually glide on wind currents. They can glide 20 ft (6 m) above the surface of the water.

58 **S**ea snakes are the most venomous snakes.

59 **A** scallop swims by quickly clapping its shell open and shut. This makes a water jet that pushes the scallop along.

60 **S**ome captive octopuses have learned to open jars containing food. Many aquariums now give their octopuses puzzles and other games to keep them from getting bored.

Oscar, an octopus with plenty of time on his hands, contemplates an escape from the tank.

61 **A** fox will sometimes nip at the heels of cattle to make the cattle run. The cattle's stomping sends mice and other rodents out of the ground for the fox to eat.

62 **T**he lungfish can live out of water for as long as four years.

63 **P**olar bears have been known to swim 62 miles (100 km) without stopping.

64 **A**n ant can lift ten times its own weight.

Oh.. He's such a show off!

I know! It's not like he's the only ant who can lift ten times his own weight!

65 The Egyptian vulture eats ostrich eggs. It uses stones to crack the eggshell.

66 Salamanders breathe through their skin.

67 Farmers in England are required by law to provide their pigs with toys.

68 The horn of a rhinoceros is made of compacted hair.

69 A woodpecker can peck up to 20 times per second.

70 Kiwis mate for life. This can be up to 30 years.

71   **B**efore seahorse eggs hatch, the male seahorse carries them in a pouch on his stomach.

72   **A** shark does not have bones. Its skeleton is made of cartilage.

73   **S**quirrels cannot remember where they have hidden half of their food.

74   **T**he stegosaurus had a brain the size of a walnut.

It was always the Stegosauruses of the class that struggled in PHYSICS because of their walnut-sized brains.

75   **A**n octopus has three hearts.

76   **T**he praying mantis is the only insect that can turn its head.

77 **A** penguin can drink salt water because it has a gland in its throat that removes the salt from the water.

78 **T**here are more plastic flamingos in the USA than real ones.

79 **A** giraffe has the same number of vertebrae in its neck as a mouse.

80 **T**urkeys often look up at the sky during a rainstorm. Unfortunately, some have drowned as a result.

81 **T**he Loch Ness monster is a protected animal under Scottish law.

82 **A** monkey was made a corporal in the South African army during World War II.

83 **A** snail can sleep for three years.

84 **A**n adult bear can run as fast as a horse.

85 **S**heep can recognize other sheep from photographs.

86 **A** locust can eat its own weight in food in one day. A typical person eats their weight in food in about six months.

87 **B**ees have five eyes.

88 **S**harks kill about 40 people each year. This is a tiny number compared to the number of people that drown each year.

89 **H**oneybees kill more people than venomous snakes do.

90 **P**olar bears are left-handed.

91 **M**osquito repellents do not repel. The repellent blocks a mosquito's sense of smell so it does not know a person is nearby.

92 **A** zebra foal can run with the herd an hour after its birth.

93 **A** marine catfish can taste with any part of its body.

94 **A** polar bear's fur is not white, but translucent.

95 **S**ome locusts have an adult lifespan of only a few weeks, after having lived in the ground as grubs for 15 years.

After living in a hole for 15 years, I'm hungry enough to eat all the plants in the world.

96 **B**utterflies taste with their feet.

97 **F**leas that live on rats have probably killed more people than anything else because they spread bubonic plague.

Hi. What do you plan to do today?

Oh...perhaps I'll go off and bite a couple of unsuspecting people ...pass on the Black Death...wipe out half of Europe.

98 The polar bear is the only mammal with hair on the soles of its feet.

99 American President John Quincy Adams owned a pet alligator. He kept it in the East Room of the White House.

100 Female ants do all the work.

101 A cockroach can live up to two weeks with its head cut off before it starves to death.

102 Dogs can make about ten vocal sounds. Cats can make more than 100 vocal sounds.

103 **W**alruses turn pink if they stay out in the sun too long.

104 **M**ore animals are killed each year by cars than by hunters.

105 **A** beaver can hold its breath underwater for up to 45 minutes.

106 **T**here are more than 500 official breeds of dog.

107 **V**ultures have a unique defence mechanism: they vomit on their enemies.

108 **A** female pigeon cannot lay an egg unless she sees another pigeon. If another pigeon is not available, her own reflection in a mirror will do.

109 Female canaries cannot sing.

110 Cockroaches could survive a nuclear holocaust because radiation does not affect them as much as it affects other species.

111 The embryos of tiger sharks fight each other while in their mother's womb. Only the survivor is born.

112 Some lizards use their lungs to help them hear. Sound makes the lizard's chest vibrate. The vibrations are carried by air from the lungs to the lizard's head where they are heard.

113 **O**rang-utans protect their territory by burping loudly to warn off intruders.

114 **F**rogs can vomit. A frog vomits its stomach first, so that its stomach is dangling out of its mouth. Then the frog uses its forearms to dig out the stomach's contents. Then the frog swallows its stomach again.

115 **A**ustralian earthworms can grow up to 10 ft (3 m) in length.

No Eric! NOT THE CARTWHEEL!

Not content with being able to stand on his head... Eric the elephant attempted more difficult gymnastic exercises with disastrous consequences.

116 **E**lephants and humans are the only animals that can stand on their heads.

117 **T**here is enough poison in a poison-arrow frog to kill 2200 people.

This isn't looking good... for me...or for whoever I'm being shot at.

118 **A** camel can drink up to 30 gallons (136 litres) of water at one time.

119 **R**ats and horses cannot vomit.

120 **R**acehorses can wear out new horseshoes in just one race.

121 **M**innows have teeth in their throat.

122 **I**f a starfish is cut into pieces, each piece will become another starfish.

123 **A** dolphin can hear sound underwater from 15 miles (24 km) away.

124 **A** scallop has 35 eyes.

125 **S**ome chimpanzees and orang-utans have been taught human sign language.

126 **M**ost insects are deaf.

127 **B**efore dolphins begin any group action, the pod holds a meeting. Each animal gets a chance to vocalize until a decision is made.

128 **S**nails produce a sticky discharge that forms a protective layer under them as they crawl. The discharge is so effective that a snail can crawl along the edge of a razor blade without cutting itself.

129 **E**arthworms have five hearts.

130 **A**ll pet hamsters are descended from one pregnant female found in the wild in 1930.

131 **S**ome reptiles have eyes that operate independently of each other, so that the animal can see in two directions at once.

132 **G**roups of sea otters tie themselves together with kelp so they do not drift apart while they sleep.

133 **A** camel's hump stores fat, not water.

134 **N**either emus nor kangaroos can walk backward.

135 Cats hate lemons.

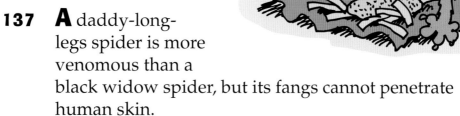

136 The tusks of the woolly mammoth were 16 ft (5 m) long.

137 A daddy-long-legs spider is more venomous than a black widow spider, but its fangs cannot penetrate human skin.

138 Camels will spit if annoyed.

139 Bees are born fully grown.

Ninety-one Funny Phobias

140 **A**blutophobia is the fear of bathing.

141 **A**carophobia is the fear of itching.

142 **A**gyrophobia is the fear of streets or crossing the street.

143 **A**lektorophobia is the fear of chickens.

Bob's irrational fear of chickens even went as far as the 5 PIECE CHICKEN MEAL DEAL (with a FREE DRINK)...at the local chicken takeaway.

144 **A**lliumphobia is the fear of garlic.

145 **A**mensiophobia is the fear of amnesia.

146 **A**nablepophobia is the fear of looking up.

147 **A**nemophobia is the fear of wind.

148 **A**peirophobia is the fear of infinity.

Arnold's fear of looking up eventually became his undoing...

I don't like the look of that shadow...! Without looking up...I think it looks like a .....

149 **A**rachibutyrophobia is the fear of peanut butter sticking to the roof of the mouth.

150 **A**utomysophobia is the fear of being dirty.

I think I've got a fear of being dirty!

How are you going to handle that? You're a pig! That's what pigs do!

151 **B**arophobia is the fear of gravity.

152 **B**asiphobia is the fear of walking.

153 **B**ibliophobia is the fear of books.

154 **B**ogyphobia is the fear of bogeys or the bogeyman.

155 **B**romidrosi-phobia is the fear of body odor.

156 **C**haetophobia is the fear of hair.

157 **C**hrometophobia is the fear of money.

158 **C**hronophobia is the fear of time.

159 **C**linophobia is the fear of going to bed.

160 **C**oimetrophobia is the fear of cemeteries.

161 **C**oulrophobia is the fear of clowns.

162 **C**yberphobia is the fear of computers or working on computers.

163 **C**yclophobia is the fear of bicycles.

164 **D**ecidophobia is the fear of making decisions.

165 **D**oraphobia is the fear of fur.

166 **E**cophobia is the fear of home.

After being diagnosed with a fear of bicycles... twin brothers Eric and Edward... also known as 'The Bicycle Brothers'... resorted to other forms of wheeled transport... and felt much better for it.

167 **E**metophobia is the fear of vomiting.

No matter how hard they tried, Terry's friends could not make him vomit. For he had a fear of vomiting.

168 **G**eniophobia is the fear of chins.

169 **G**enuphobia is the fear of knees.

170 **G**eumaphobia is the fear of taste.

171 **G**nosiophobia is the fear of knowledge.

172 **G**ymnophobia is the fear of being naked.

173 **H**eliophobia is the fear of the sun.

174 **I**deophobia is the fear of ideas.

175 **K**leptophobia is the fear of stealing.

176 **K**oinoniphobia is the fear of rooms.

177 **K**oniophobia is the fear of dust.

178 **L**achanophobia is the fear of vegetables.

179 **L**eukophobia is the fear of the color white.

180 **L**ogophobia is the fear of words.

181 Lutraphobia is the fear of otters.

182 Macrophobia is the fear of long waits.

Mr Jones the friendly Station Master broke the bad news carefully to Edward (who had a fear of waiting) ...that his train service had been discontinued.

183 Meteorophobia is the fear of meteors.

184 Microphobia is the fear of small things.

185 Mnemophobia is the fear of memories.

186 Myrmecophobia is the fear of ants.

187 **M**yxophobia is the fear of slimy things.

188 **N**ebulaphobia is the fear of fog.

Fearing a thick fog entering his loungeroom and engulfing him while sleeping infront of the TV... ...Harold closed all doors and windows...but failed to close Harry the cat's cat flap in the back door.

189 **N**ephophobia is the fear of clouds.

190 **N**omatophobia is the fear of names.

191 **N**umerophobia is the fear of numbers.

192 **O**chophobia is the fear of vehicles.

A fear of vehicles drove Shirley to start a movement to bring back the HORSE for transport.

HORSE POWER is great! BRING BACK THE HORSE?

Give JOBS to out of work HORSES

I've been unemployed standing around eating grass in a paddock for five years!

193 **O**mbrophobia is the fear of rain.

Due to his irrational fear of rain, Alex spent two days pinned to a wall under an awning waiting for the low pressure storm cell to leave his country.

194 **O**mmetaphobia is the fear of eyes.

195 **O**rnithophobia is the fear of birds.

196 **P**agophobia is the fear of ice or frost.

197 **P**apyrophobia is the fear of paper.

198 **P**araskavedekatriaphobia is the fear of Friday the 13th.

199 **P**edophobia is the fear of children.

200   **P**eladophobia is the fear of bald people.

201   **P**hagophobia is the fear of eating or swallowing.

202   **P**hilophobia is the fear of falling in love.

Esmerelda's fear of love was thinly disguised as a lack of interest.

203   **P**honophobia is the fear of noise.

204   **P**hotophobia is the fear of light.

205 **P**lutophobia is the fear of wealth.

206 **P**neumatophobia is the fear of air.

207 **P**ogonophobia is the fear of beards.

I suppose someone with a fear of AIR must just... ...hold their breath!

BIG BEARD CONVENTION

So this isn't the MODEL RAILWAY CONVENTION? For someone with a love for model trains...and a fear of beards...this is the WRONG place to be!

208 **P**teronophobia is the fear of being tickled with feathers.

209 **R**anidaphobia is the fear of frogs.

210 **R**upophobia is the fear of dirt.

211 **S**amhainophobia is the fear of Halloween.

212 **S**elenophobia is the fear of the moon.

213 **S**omniphobia is the fear of sleep.

214 **S**ymmetro-phobia is the fear of symmetry.

215 **S**yngenesophobia is the fear of relatives.

216 **T**aphephobia is the fear of being buried alive.

217 **T**eratophobia is the fear of monsters.

218 **T**onsurophobia is the fear of haircuts.

219 **T**remophobia is the fear of trembling.

Jimmy quickly changed the subject to draw attention away from the fact that because of a fear of haircuts...he'd never had a haircut in his life.

220 **T**riskaidekaphobia is the fear of the number 13.

221 **U**ranophobia is the fear of urine or urinating.

222 **V**estiphobia is the fear of clothing.

223 **V**itricophobia is the fear of step-fathers.

224 **X**anthophobia is the fear of the color yellow.

225 **X**enophobia is the fear of strangers or foreigners.

226 **Z**elophobia is the fear of jealousy.

227 **Z**emmiphobia is the fear of the great mole rat.

228 **Z**oophobia is the fear of animals.

And finally…

229 **P**hobophobia is the fear of fear.

230 **P**anophobia is the fear of everything.

George hid under his pillow when his fear of everything got to him…

Wacky World Records

VOSTOK...ANTARTICA 21 JULY 1983

231 The coldest temperature recorded on Earth was –129°F (–89°C) at Vostok, Antarctica, on July 21 1983.

232 Charles Osborne had the hiccups for 68 years.

233 The world record for most jumps on a pogo-stick is 206 864 jumps.

234 Bhutan was the last country to get the telephone. It did not have one until 1981.

235 The largest iceberg was sighted in the South Pacific Ocean in 1956. It was 208 miles (332 km) long and 60 miles (96 km) wide, or about the size of Belgium.

How much ice did you need in your drink my dear?

I've brought back enough to cover Belgium.

236 The tallest tree in the world, a coast redwood, is 397.1 ft (115.55 m) tall.

237 The longest kiss lasted 50 hours, 25 minutes and 1 second.

Just imagine a treehouse up there!

238 The biggest palace in the world is the Imperial Palace in Beijing. It has so many rooms that you could sleep in a different room every night for 25 years.

239 The longest trip in a wave-powered boat was 3780 nautical miles (7000 kms).

240 Although covered with ice, Antarctica is the driest place on the planet with humidity lower than the Gobi Desert.

241 For 110 years, the USA was the world's top manufacturing nation. It was overtaken by China in 2010.

242 The longest time spent standing on one foot is 76 hours, 40 minutes.

243 In Great Britain, the most dangerous sport is gardening. Twenty per cent of all accidents there occur in the garden.

244 The biggest pumpkin weighed 1725 lb (782 kg).

245 The warmest temperature recorded on Earth was 136°F (57.8°C) at El Azizia, Libya, on September 13 1922. Bath water is considered scalding at 125°F (46°C).

246 The longest nose belonged to Thomas Wedders. It measured 7.5 in (19 cm). Thomas worked in a freak show in the 1770s.

247 The longest place name is "Bangkok" in Thai. It is: Krungthep Mahanakhon Bovorn Ratanakosin Mahintharayutthaya Mahadilokpop Noparatratchathani Burirom Udomratchanivet Mahasathan Amornpiman Avatarnsathit Sakkathattiyavisnukarmprasit. It means "City of Angels." It is usually shortened to Krungthep Mahanakhon, for obvious reasons.

Mm! Mmmmm m m'mmm m mm OUCH! Mm mmm mm OUCH...mm mm mmmm (TRANSLATED) Look! I'm going to have to call you back...OUCH! ...I'm in a competition trying to ...OUCH...stuff as many live scorpions into my mouth as I can.

248 The record for the most scorpions held in the mouth at one time is 22.

249 The first automobile race in the USA was held in Chicago in 1895. The track ran from Chicago to Evanston, Illinois. The winner was J. Frank Duryea, whose average speed was 7.5 miles (12 km) per hour.

250 The largest crater on the moon is also the largest impact crater in the solar system. It measures 1300 miles (2100 km) across.

251 Strongman John Evans holds the world record for the heaviest weight balanced only on his head. He balanced 101 bricks that weighed 416 lb (188 kg).

Ooh! Sorry! I figured it was only one more little brick!

Brian felt responsible for ruining John's world record attempt at balancing bricks on his head...by adding the 102nd brick.

252 The largest pearl ever found was the size of a tennis ball.

253 The fastest wind speed recorded was 318 miles (508 km) per hour in Oklahoma on May 3 1999.

254 The largest known volcano is Olympus Mons on Mars. It is 370 miles (590 km) wide and 79 000 ft (24 000 m) high. It is almost three times higher than Mount Everest.

255 The Holy See (State of the Vatican City) in Rome, Italy, is the smallest sovereign state in the world. It has a population of less than 1000 people.

256 The youngest graduate got his bachelor's degree in 1994 at the age of ten years, five months.

257 Dorothy Straight's first book, *How The World Began*, was published in 1964 when she was six years old, making her the youngest ever published author.

258 The most powerful computer in the world is the Sequoia supercomputer at Lawrence Livermore National Library. It weighs about the same as 30 elephants and can do 16.3 quadrillion calculations per second, which translates to 16.3 petaflops per second.

259 The lightest person weighed 13 lb (6 kg) on her twentieth birthday.

260 Jon Brower Minnoch of Seattle weighed 1400 lb (634 kg) when he was admitted to hospital. After 16 months, Minnoch was discharged at 476 lb (215 kg).

261 The oldest cockroach fossil is about 280 million years old, which means the cockroach lived 80 million years before the first dinosaurs.

262 The loudest burp was 107.1 decibels (think jet airplane).

263 The record for holding one's breath underwater is 22 minutes.

264 The world record for pole sitting is 196 days on an 8 ft (2.5 m) pole.

265 The only time on record that snow has fallen in the Sahara Desert was on February 18 1979. The storm lasted half an hour and the snow soon melted.

Abdul and his friend Ali didn't want to miss any of the brief half hour snow season over the Sahara Desert in 1979... so were ready to go.

266 Golf is the only sport that has been played on the moon.

267 The shortest war in history was fought between Zanzibar and England in 1896. The war had lasted for just 38 minutes when Zanzibar surrendered.

268 The longest recorded flight of a chicken is 13 seconds.

269 More baked beans are eaten in Great Britain than in any other country.

270 The world's smallest tree is the dwarf willow. It grows to 2 in (5 cm) on the tundra of Greenland.

271 The oldest known living thing is a bristlecone pine called Methuselah. It is located in the White Mountains on the California–Nevada border. The tree is estimated to be 4767 years old.

A Greenlander about to flatten a whole forest of dwarf willows in one step!

Hey Dad! Wait until you see what we've got! We've got us... A CHRISTMAS TREE!

Chucky brings home the 4767-year-old Bristlecone pine after a hiking trip to the White Mountains of USA.

272 The Guinness Book of Records holds the record for being the book most often stolen from public libraries.

273 The world's youngest parents were eight and nine years old and lived in 1910.

274 **A**ir hostess Vesna Vulovic of Yugoslavia fell 33 330 ft (10 160 m) from an airplane into a snowbound forest in Serbska Kamenice, Czechoslovakia, on January 26 1972. It was the longest fall a person has survived.

It's Only Natural

275 **W**atermelons are grown square in Japan so they take up less space and are easier to stack.

276 **A**n apple, potato, and onion all taste sweet if you eat them with your nose plugged.

277 **J**upiter is bigger than all the other planets in our solar system combined.

278 **H**ot water is heavier than cold water.

279 **N**atural gas has no smell. The smell is added for safety reasons.

280 **R**esearch indicates that plants grow better when they are stroked.

281 **S**trawberries contain more vitamin C than oranges.

282 **F**orty-one percent of the moon is not visible from Earth at any time.

While Olive stroked most of her plants to make them grow... Her very prickly cactii remained stunted in the corner of the greenhouse.

WHAT REALLY HAPPENS ON THE 41% OF THE MOON WE CAN'T SEE FROM EARTH.

283 **P**ollen never deteriorates. It is one of the few natural substances that lasts indefinitely.

284 **A** blue moon is the second full moon within a single calendar month.

285 The age of the universe is 13.75 billion years.

THE UNIVERSE TURNS 13.75 BILLION

286 Because of the rotation of the Earth, an object can be thrown farther if it is thrown west.

287 Ninety percent of all extinct species are birds.

WHY 90% OF ALL EXTINCT SPECIES ...ARE BIRDS!

288 Sound travels through water three times faster than through air.

289 True berries include the grape, tomato, and eggplant, but not the raspberry or blackberry.

290 **P**earls dissolve in vinegar.

291 **T**he largest flower in the world is the corpse flower or *Rafflesia*. It grows up to 4 ft (1.2 m) wide and it stinks.

292 **T**here are eight peas per pod on average.

293 **I**n Calama, a town in the Atacama Desert of Chile, it has never rained.

294 **R**aindrops are not really shaped like drops; they are perfectly round.

295 **L**emons contain more sugar than strawberries.

296 **W**hen scientists drilled through the ice of Antarctica's Lake Vanda, they discovered that the water at the bottom of the lake was an amazingly warm 77°F (24°C). Ice crystals heat the water by focusing light onto the bottom of the lake.

297 **T**he Amazon rainforest makes one-fifth of the world's oxygen.

298 **T**he Antarctic ice sheet contains 71 percent of the world's fresh water.

299 **A** tomato is a fruit, not a vegetable.

The Amazon rainforest makes ⅕ of the world's oxygen. What's not quite as well known is that it also makes a good percentage of the world's fish that can eat you... snakes that can crush you and natives that can kill you!

Freddy tried the... 'Did you know the TOMATO was a fruit trick' on his friends almost every week... and they were beginning to tire of it.

300 **L**ettuce is part of the sunflower family.

301 **W**ater is the only substance on Earth that is lighter as a solid than as a liquid.

302 **C**oconuts kill more people than sharks do. Approximately 150 people are killed each year by coconuts.

303 **A**ntarctica is the only place on Earth that is not owned by any country.

304 **T**he liquid inside young coconuts can be used as a substitute for blood plasma.

305 **T**he only food that does not spoil is honey.

306 **A**ustralia is the only continent on Earth without an active volcano.

307 **F**ingernails grow nearly four times faster than toenails.

308 **T**he apple, the almond, and the peach are all members of the rose family.

309 **B**y raising your legs slowly and lying on your back, you cannot sink in quicksand.

310 **C**hina has a beverage called white tea. It is simply boiled water.

311 It is impossible to sneeze with your eyes open.

312 Venus is the only planet that rotates clockwise.

313 On February 20 1943 in a cornfield near the village of Paricutin, Mexico, the ground cracked open and began to spew red-hot rocks. A volcano was born. It grew to 35 ft (10.6 m) the first day. By 1952, it had soared to 1352 ft (412 m) and had buried two towns.

314 The white oak does not produce acorns until it is about 50 years old.

Crunching Numbers

315 Buckingham Palace has more than 600 rooms.

316 The opposite sides of a dice always add up to seven.

317 Woodpecker scalps, porpoise teeth, and giraffe tails have all been used as money.

318 A bag of potato chips costs 200 times more than the same weight in potatoes.

319 **A** jiffy is an actual unit of time. It is 1/100 of a second.

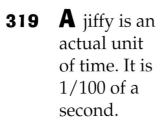

320 **T**here are more than 1267 million telephone lines in the world.

321 **T**he average office worker uses about 10 000 sheets of paper each year.

322 **T**wenty percent of all road accidents in Sweden involve a moose.

Twenty percent of all road accidents in Sweden involve a MOOSE.

323 **T**here are more than 200 lashes on a human eyelid. Each lash is shed every three to five months.

324 **M**ore than 2100 languages are spoken in Africa.

325 An ostrich egg takes four hours to hard-boil.

326 A porcupine has about 30 000 quills.

327 More than 80 billion aspirins are sold each year.

328 Humans have 639 muscles, but caterpillars have more than 4000.

329 If you could drive to the sun at 55 miles (90 km) per hour, it would take about 193 years.

330 A baby is born in the USA every seven seconds.

331 Today, 80 percent of the world's zippers are made in the Qiaotou factory in China.

332 **J**ust 20 seconds' worth of fuel remained when Apollo 11's lunar module landed on the moon.

All it took was a 20 second dispute over where to land to turn the first landing on the moon into the first crash on the moon!

333 **U**p to 10 in (25 cm) of rain can fall on a rainforest in a single day.

334 **A** solar day on Mercury, from sunrise to sunset, lasts about six Earth months.

335 **T**he amniotic fluid that surrounds a baby in the womb is completely replaced every three hours.

336 There are more than 40 000 varieties of rice.

337 Cats can spend 16 hours a day sleeping.

338 A bee needs to flap its wings 250 times per second to remain in the air.

After what amounted to sleeping most of the day, Harry the Persian slept most of the night catching up on the sleep he missed during the day.

339 Eighty-three percent of American adults own a cell phone.

340 It takes 72 muscles to speak one word.

341 In the first eight months of his presidency, George W. Bush was on vacation 42 percent of the time.

342 **A**n alligator has 80 teeth.

343 **I**t takes approximately 850 peanuts to make a standard jar of peanut butter.

344 **T**here are about five million grains in a packet of sugar.

345 **T**he Great Wall Of China is 2149 miles (3460 km) long.

346 **S**ummer and winter on Uranus each last 21 Earth years.

347 **T**here are 113 Bibles sold every minute.

348 There are roughly 22 million active stamp collectors in the USA.

349 Every day, McDonald's serves about 68 million customers in 119 countries.

350 The weight of all bacteria in the world is equal to the weight of all plants on Earth.

351 There are 2.5 million rivets in the Eiffel Tower.

352 The Earth travels around the Sun at about 67 000 miles (107 000 km) per hour.

Pierre the Rivet Counter at the Eiffel Tower loses count while counting rivets ...

353 The burrowing rate of the gopher is equivalent to a human digging a tunnel 18 in (45 cm) wide and 7 miles (11 km) long in ten hours.

354 Close to four billion movie tickets are sold in India every year.

355 One in five children in the world has never been inside a schoolroom.

356 One ragweed plant can release one billion grains of pollen per year.

357 On average, 90 acres of pizza are eaten every day in the USA.

358 **A** dragonfly lives for one day.

359 **T**here are more insects in a 1 mile (1.6 km) square of rural land than there are people on the planet.

A dragonfly lives for one day...
...that's 24 hours...
WHOOPS! Time's up!

DON'T MOVE SHIRLEY OLD GIRL!
Do you realise that if you do....
you might squash more bugs than there are people in China!

360 **T**he largest American bill is for $100 000.

361 **T**he human heart creates enough pressure to squirt blood over 30 ft (9 m).

362 **A** dairy cow will give about 200 000 glasses of milk in its lifetime.

Oh...what did you do to yourself?
You've cut your finger!
Let's get a dressing on
that little bleeder.

363 Chamoy Thipyaso was convicted of fraud and sentenced to 141 078 years in a Thai prison.

364 The main library at Indiana University sinks over 1 in (2.5 cm) every year. When it was built, engineers failed to take into account the weight of the books that would occupy the building.

The library at Indiana University finally sinks under the weight of the books after C.J. returns his three overdue library books.

365 The first product to have its barcode scanned was a pack of Wrigley's gum.

366 There are 18 doctors in the USA called Dr. Doctor, and one called Dr. Surgeon.

367 One 75-watt bulb gives more light than three 25-watt bulbs.

368 Twenty thousand men took 22 years to build the Taj Mahal.

369 **B**olivia has two capital cities.

370 **T**he American government holds nearly three percent of all the gold refined through history. Most of it is at Fort Knox.

371 **A** Weddell seal can hold its breath underwater for seven hours.

372 **I**n America, every major league baseball team buys about 20 000 baseballs a year.

373 **T**he height of the Eiffel Tower varies by as much as 6 in (15 cm), depending on the temperature.

374 Mickey Mouse received 800 000 pieces of fan mail in 1933.

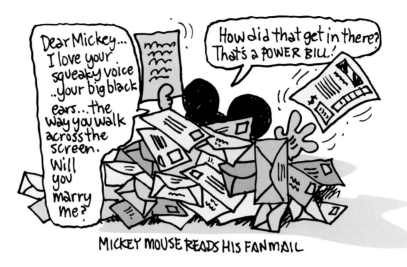

MICKEY MOUSE READS HIS FANMAIL

375 The blue whale, the largest animal ever, is 100 ft (30 m) long. It weighs as much as four large dinosaurs, 23 elephants, 230 cows, or 1800 men.

376 The name Hitler was listed 22 times in the New York phone book before World War II. After the war, the name was not listed once.

377 Almost one-quarter of all mammal species on Earth are bats.

Bats make up one quarter of all mammals on Earth...
And Juan finds the cave in Bolivia where they all live.

378 Lightning is five times hotter than the surface of the sun.

379 The average American over 50 will have spent five years waiting in lines.

380 The Earth is 4.54 billion years old.

381 The search engine Google got its name from the word "googol", which is the number one with a hundred zeros after it.

382 The largest hotel in the world in 2002 was the MGM Grand in Las Vegas, Nevada, with 5034 rooms.

383 Wearing headphones can increase the bacteria in your ears by up to 700 times.

384 The leaves of some water lilies can be 8 ft (2.4 m) wide.

385 It takes about 63 000 trees to make the Sunday edition of the *New York Times*.

386 It takes nearly 3000 cows to supply the USA's National Football League with enough leather to make a year's supply of footballs.

387 In Haiti, only 12 out of every 1000 people owns a car.

388 Pain travels through the human body at a speed of over 350 ft (106 m) per second.

389 The Sun makes up 99 percent of the matter in our solar system.

390 The weight of all the ants on Earth is approximately the same weight as all the people on Earth.

391 The average person spends three years of their life on the toilet.

392 There are approximately 3500 astronomers in the USA, but more than 15 000 astrologers.

393 The average number of people in aircraft over the USA in any given hour is 100 000.

394 **A** person drinks about 20 000 gallons (75 000 litres) of water in his lifetime.

395 **T**he human head contains 22 bones.

After hearing that a person drinks 20 000 gallons of water in a lifetime... Arnold decided to drink all of his share in one go and get it over and done with.

396 **L**ightning strikes the Earth 100 times every second or 6000 times every minute.

397 **Y**ou share your birthday with more than nine million people.

398 **O**ne bat can consume 1000 mosquitoes in a single hour.

399 **A**n office desk has 400 times more bacteria on it than a toilet does.

400 The average lead pencil can be used to draw a line 35 miles (56 km) long or to write approximately 50 000 English words.

30 miles into his 35 mile line Al's pencil began to run low... But fortunately for Al he had a spare pencil to finish the last 5 miles of his line. And why was he drawing a 35 mile line? Well...it was easier than writing 50,000 words the the average pencil is good for....

401 The wingspan of a Boeing 747 is longer than the Wright brothers' first flight.

Keep the nose up Wilbhur! We've got to make it across this... What is that? A big plane?

Hang on Orville. Turn off the engine. Why are we bothering to even try for the first powered flight? Somebody's already beaten us to it!

402 By weight, a hamburger costs more than a new car.

403 No piece of dry, square paper can be folded in half more than seven times.

404 More than 14 billion pencils are manufactured each year in the world. If these were placed end to end, they would circle the world 62 times.

405 Recycling one glass jar saves enough energy to power a television for three hours.

After learning on TV that recycling one glass jar could power a television for one hour... Debbie figured that gobbling down a jar of pickled onions.. a jar of anchovies and a half jar of pickled gherkins would give her at least a full day of TV.

406 If all the blood vessels in your body were placed end to end, they would make a line about 60 000 miles (96 000 km) long.

407 In one day your heart beats 100 000 times.

408 At a steady jogger's pace of six miles (10 km) per hour, it would take 173 days to go around the equatorial circumference of Earth, and more than five years to go around Jupiter, the largest planet.

OUCH! It's my sore toe. I can't go on!

Herb was forced to abandon his 173 day training run around the world after only 10 minutes blaming an ingrown toenail as the reason. His coach and manager feared his problem toe may act up on his 5 year run around the planet Jupiter.

409 The Empire State Building consists of more than 10 million bricks.

410 The longest conga had 119 986 people in it.

411 There are more than 4000 living species of cockroaches.

412 The average bank teller loses about $250 every year.

413 A human's small intestine is 20 ft (6 m) long.

414 Scientists estimate that there are at least 15 million stars for every person on Earth.

415 **A** car traveling at 100 miles (160 km) per hour would take more than 29 million years to reach the nearest star beyond the sun.

416 **T**here are ten towns named Hollywood in the USA.

417 **S**ome kinds of bamboo grow 35 in (89 cm) in one day.

418 **I**t is estimated that 6500 languages are spoken in the world today.

419 **I**n the average lifetime a person will breathe in nearly 44 lb (20 kg) of dust.

420 **Y**ou blink over 10 million times in a year.

421 The most drought-resistant tree is the boab tree. It can store 35 800 gallons (163 000 litres) of water in its trunk for later use.

It was while chopping firewood in the Outback that Jack discovered the difference between a gumtree and a Boab tree is about 35 800 gallons of water.

422 Three hundred and fifteen entries in Webster's 1996 dictionary were misspelled.

423 Rats multiply so quickly that, in 18 months, two rats could have more than one million descendants.

424 A butterfly has more than 12 000 lenses in each eye.

425 There are more cell phones than people in the USA.

426 The combined wealth of the world's 250 richest people is greater than the combined wealth of the poorest 1.5 billion people.

427 The first number plates were introduced in 1893.

428 Outer space begins 50 miles (80 km) above the Earth.

Reginald Smith pays big money for the first number plate in 1893 and receives the first speeding ticket soon after.

429 When awake, cats spend up to 30 percent of their time grooming.

Rex...always an excessive cat as a kitten, was not content with the average 30% of his time spent grooming...He went for the full 100%

430 A woodchuck breathes only ten times per hour while hibernating. An active woodchuck breathes 2100 times per hour.

431 An elephant can smell water nearly 3 miles (5 km) away.

432 Linen can absorb up to 20 times its weight in moisture before it feels damp.

433 During a typical human life, a heart will beat approximately 2.5 billion times.

434 In 1956, 80 percent of American households had a refrigerator compared to only eight percent of British households.

435 A hippopotamus can open its mouth 4 ft (1.2 m) wide.

436 The sperm whale's intestines are over 450 ft (137 m) long.

437 **N**icaragua had 396 different rulers between 1839 and 1855; their average reign lasted less than 15 days.

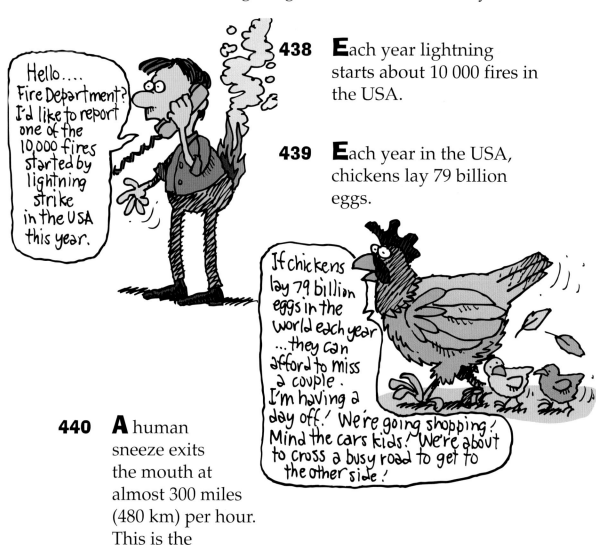

Hello....
Fire Department?
I'd like to report
one of the
10,000 fires
started by
lightning
strike
in the USA
this year.

If chickens
lay 79 billion
eggs in the
world each year
...they can
afford to miss
a couple.
I'm having a
day off! We're going shopping!
Mind the cars kids! We're about
to cross a busy road to get to
the other side!

438 **E**ach year lightning starts about 10 000 fires in the USA.

439 **E**ach year in the USA, chickens lay 79 billion eggs.

440 **A** human sneeze exits the mouth at almost 300 miles (480 km) per hour. This is the speed of the wind in a class five tornado.

441 **T**here is the same amount of water in 10 in (25 cm) of snow as in 1 in (2.5 cm) of rain.

442 **T**he fastest moon in our solar system circles Jupiter once every seven hours. It travels faster than 70 000 miles (112 000 km) per hour.

443 The largest jellyfish ever found was 7.5 ft (2.3 m) long.

444 A Boeing 747 airplane holds 57 285 gallons (260 000 litres) of fuel.

445 Besides inventing the telephone, Alexander Graham Bell set a world water speed record of 70 miles (113 km) per hour in a hydrofoil boat.

446 The estimated number of M&Ms sold each day in the USA is 200 million.

447 There are approximately 31.5 million seconds in a year.

448 It takes six months to build a Rolls Royce and 13 hours to build a Toyota.

449 The moon has no atmosphere, so footprints left there by astronauts should remain for at least 10 million years.

450 The oldest fish in captivity lived to 88 years of age.

451 If you stretch out a standard slinky, it measures 87 ft (26.5 m).

452 Around 10 percent of all the people who ever lived are alive today.

453 **O**n average, 100 people choke to death on ballpoint pens every year.

454 **T**here are 2 598 960 five-card hands possible in a 52-card deck of cards.

455 **T**he cruise liner, the QE2, moves only 6 in (15 cm) for each 1 gallon (4.5 litres) of diesel that it burns.

Entertainment and the Arts

456 **W**hen an orange is shown in any of *The Godfather* movies, it means a character is about to die or have a close call.

457 **"T**winkle Twinkle Little Star" was written by Mozart.

458 **W**hen young and poor, Pablo Picasso kept warm by burning his own paintings.

It's my greatest work yet! It's about lots of little stars twinkling brightly in the sky at night over Austria. Something kids can sing along to. I'll call my masterpiece... TWINKLE TWINKLE LITTLE STAR.

After gazing at the night sky for ten minutes Mozart comes up with a great idea.

459 The first time a toilet was shown on television was in the show "Leave It to Beaver."

460 Charlie Chaplin once received 73 000 pieces of fan mail in three days.

461 Director George Lucas had trouble getting funding for the movie *Star Wars* because most film studios thought people would not go and see it.

462 No one knows where Mozart is buried.

463 Mel Blanc, who was the voice of Bugs Bunny, was allergic to carrots. He had to chew a carrot for a take, then spit it into a bucket.

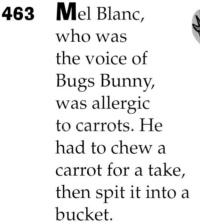

464 Leonardo da Vinci spent 12 years painting *Mona Lisa's* lips.

465 **W**alt Disney was afraid of mice.

466 **B**arbie's full name is Barbara Millicent Roberts.

467 **T**he first toy advertized on television was Mr. Potato Head.

468 **B**ecause metal was scarce, the Oscars given out during World War II were made of wood.

469 **S**herlock Holmes never said "Elementary, my dear Watson."

470 **T**he most popular movie star in 1925 was the dog Rin Tin Tin.

471 **M**arcel the monkey was fired from the television show "Friends" because of his nasty habit of vomiting live worms.

472 **S**occer is the most popular sport in the world.

473 **P**inocchio is Italian for "pine eyes."

474 **T**he shortest television commercial was one-quarter of a second long.

475 **"W**hite Christmas" sung by Bing Crosby has sold over 100 million records, making it the most popular recording of all time.

476 In 1935, a writer named Dudley Nichols refused to accept the Oscar for his screenplay *The Informer* because the Writers' Guild was on strike.

477 In 1970, George C. Scott refused the Best Actor Oscar for *Patton*.

478 In 1972, Marlon Brando refused the Oscar for his role in *The Godfather*.

479 In *Casablanca*, Humphrey Bogart never said "Play it again, Sam."

480 Donald Duck comics were once banned in Finland because Donald does not wear pants.

Donald Duck receives pants from fans in Finland to stop bans on his comics....

481 *Tom Sawyer* was the first novel written on a typewriter.

Author Mark Twain gives up the fountain pen and wrestles with new technology.

482 The largest book ever published is *Bhutan: A Visual Odyssey Across the Kingdom*. The book is 5 x 7 ft (1.5 x 2.1 m). It has 112 pages and weighs 133 lb (60 kg).

483 In Mel Brooks' *Silent Movie*, mime Marcel Marceau is the only person who has a speaking role.

484 The Bible has been translated into Klingon.

485 Boxing is the most popular theme in movies about sport.

Max makes a big mistake in believing the movie 'The Ring' was going to be a fantasy.

486 The world's longest-running play is *The Mousetrap*. It is a murder mystery that was written by Agatha Christie in 1947. It has been performed over 20 000 times.

487 In the 1991 Disney film *Beauty and the Beast*, one sign in the forest points to a place called Anaheim. Another sign points down a dark, sinister-looking path to Valencia. Anaheim is actually the site of Disneyland, while the rival Six Flags Magic Mountain amusement theme park is in the city of Valencia.

488 The first four countries to have television were England, the USA, the USSR, and Brazil.

THE DAY **BEFORE** TELEVISION STARTED IN BRITAIN

489 Donald Duck's middle name is Fauntleroy.

490 The song "Rudolph the Red-Nosed Reindeer" was invented in 1939 for a department store promotion.

491 "The Muppet Show" was banned in Saudi Arabia because one of its stars was a pig.

492 Alfred Hitchcock did not have a belly button. It was eliminated when he was sewn up after surgery.

493 Virginia Woolf wrote all her books standing up.

494 The characters Bert and Ernie on "Sesame Street" were named after Bert the cop and Ernie the taxi driver in Frank Capra's *It's a Wonderful Life*.

495 Before the 1960s, men with long hair were not allowed to enter Disneyland.

496 One of the biggest box-office flops was Kevin Costner's *Waterworld*, which cost more than $200 million.

497 Whoopi Goldberg's real name is Caryn Elaine Johnson.

498 Drew Carey once worked at Denny's.

499 The King of Hearts is the only king in a deck of cards with a mustache.

Nigel found to his surprise that in the deck of cards only the King of Hearts had a moustache. So with a quick flick of the felt pen ...everyone had a moustache ...and eyes...and hair...lots of hair...all of it black.

500 Mark Twain, one of America's best-loved authors, dropped out of school when he was 12 years old, after his father died.

501 Dolly Parton once lost a Dolly Parton lookalike contest.

502 In 1938, the creators of Superman sold the rights to the character for $65 each.

503 During the chariot scene in *Ben Hur,* a small red car can be seen in the background.

Mario takes a wrong turn into the supermarket carpark and parks his little red car on the set of Ben Hur instead.

504 There were 47 Charlie Chan movies. Six different actors played the role, but none of them was Chinese.

505 Vincent Van Gogh only sold one painting in his life and that was to his brother.

506 Debra Winger was the voice of ET.

507 More Monopoly money than real money is printed in a year.

508 The first time a toilet was flushed in a movie was in *Psycho*.

509 **S**onny and Cher originally called themselves Caesar and Cleo.

510 **I**n Finland, Cinderella is known as Tuna.

511 **X**-rays of the *Mona Lisa* show that there are three completely different versions, all painted by Leonardo da Vinci, under the final portrait.

X-Rays of the Mona Lisa reveal previous versions underneath!

512 **W**arren Beatty and Shirley Maclaine are brother and sister.

513 **T**he sound effect of ET walking was made by someone squishing jelly in her hands.

514   Every time Beethoven sat down to write music, he poured cold water over his head.

515   The longest non-talking film ever made was Andy Warhol's *Sleep*. It consists solely of a man sleeping for eight hours.

516   The quietest piece of music in the world is John Cage's "3 minutes and 27 seconds," which consists of a person sitting in front of a piano for that length of time, then leaving.

517   Leonardo da Vinci could write with one hand and draw with the other at the same time.

It's well known that Leonardo Da Vinci could use both hands at the same time to write and draw... but he may have also been able to balance a small leather ball on his nose while tapping his foot to Italian folk tunes as well!

518 The first CD pressed in the USA was Bruce Springsteen's "Born in the USA."

519 During the eighteenth century, books that were considered offensive were sometimes whipped.

520 The idea of a countdown before a rocket launch originated as a tension-building device in the 1929 movie *The Woman on the Moon.*

521 The people of Iceland read more books per capita than any other people in the world.

522 In every episode of "Seinfeld," there is a Superman.

523 The name of Oz in the *Wizard of Oz* was thought up by the creator, Frank Baum, when he looked at his filing and saw O-Z.

What the WIZARD OF OZ might have been called if Frank hadn't taken a few minutes more to think about the title and not glanced upon the O-Z file of his filing cabinet.

524 The first film with spoken dialogue premiered on October 6 1927 in New York. It was *The Jazz Singer* starring Al Jolson.

525 John Travolta turned down the starring roles in *An Officer and a Gentleman* and *Tootsie*.

526 Whoopi Goldberg was a mortuary cosmetologist and a bricklayer before becoming an actress.

527 Many of the details we associate with Santa Claus were invented for a Coca Cola advertizing campaign around 1890.

YO HO HO HO... OOOOHH! ...oh my!

Santa realises he's had one too many colas from his lifetime supply given to him for starring in an advertizing campaign in 1890.

528 In most television commercials that show milk, advertizing milk (a mixture of white paint and a little thinner) is used in place of real milk.

529 Humphrey Bogart was related to Princess Diana. They were seventh cousins.

530 The longest movie runs for 85 hours and is fittingly titled *The Cure for Insomnia*.

Bob fell asleep 84½ hours into the 85 hour movie ... 'THE CURE FOR INSOMNIA' ...and missed the ending!

Sixty-nine Ludicrous Laws

Many of these laws date back to a time when the ideals they represented were commonly accepted. Some are still in place today because the local authorities have not bothered to remove them yet.

531 **P**acific Grove, California: It is a misdemeanor to kill or threaten a butterfly.

532 **V**entura County, California: Cats or dogs cannot mate without a permit.

Don't touch the butterfly dear! We don't want you doing time in a state run penitentiary with hardened criminals! Remember we have tough butterfly laws in this state.

533 Sarasota, Florida: It is illegal to wear swimwear while singing in a public place.

534 Illinois: It is illegal to give lighted cigars to dogs, cats, or other pets.

535 Chicago, Illinois: A hatpin is considered a concealed weapon.

536 Florida: Men may not be seen publicly in any kind of strapless gown.

537 Belgium: Every child must learn the harmonica at primary school.

538 Florida: If an elephant is left tied to a parking meter, the parking fee has to be paid.

539 Minnesota: It is illegal to mock skunks.

540 Michigan: It is illegal for a woman to cut her hair without her husband's consent.

541 Florida: Unmarried women are prohibited from parachuting on Sundays.

542 Alabama: It is illegal to wear a fake mustache that causes laughter in church.

Despite sitting in the very back row of the church...
Charlie realised he'd been sprung wearing a fake mustache.

543 Bellingham, Washington: It was once illegal for a woman to take more than three steps backward while dancing.

544 Brainerd, Minnesota: Every man must grow a beard.

545 **O**hio: It is illegal to sell beer while wearing a Santa Claus suit, even if you are a dog.

546 **S**eattle, Washington: It is illegal to sell lollipops, but suckers are fine.

547 **V**irginia: All bathtubs must be outside, not in the house.

Here in Virginia... we have our bathtubs outside the house. We keep our towels inside the house. And that's where my towel is right now... inside the house... not out here where I need it! I wish I had a towel!

548 **T**oronto, Canada: It is illegal to ride streetcars on Sundays after eating garlic.

DING-DING   DING-DING

This is Sergeant Bottecelli from the Garlic Breath Squad. I'd like anyone who's eaten spaghetti sauce or garlic bread today to move outside and put your hands on the side of the streetcar... and not breathe on anybody please.

549 **I**ndiana: People are not allowed to attend a movie house or theatre, nor ride in a public streetcar less than four hours after eating garlic.

550 Los Angeles: In 1838, a man had to obtain a license before serenading a woman.

551 Cleveland, Ohio: It is illegal to capture mice without a hunting license.

552 Arizona: It is illegal to hunt camels.

553 Kentucky: It is illegal to carry an ice-cream cone in your pocket.

554 Louisiana: It is illegal to rob a bank, then shoot the teller with a water pistol.

555 Indiana: It is prohibited to take a bath in the winter.

556 **K**entucky: You must take a bath at least once a year.

557 **A**laska: It is illegal to look at or pursue a moose from a flying vehicle.

558 **A**tlanta, Georgia: It is illegal to tie a giraffe to a telephone pole or street lamp.

559 **I**daho: It is forbidden to give a person a box of candy that weighs more than 50 lb (23 kg).

560 **N**ew York State: It is illegal to shoot a rabbit from a trolley car.

561 **S**omalia, Africa: It is illegal to carry old gum on the tip of your nose.

562 New Jersey: It is illegal to slurp soup.

563 Milan, Italy: Citizens can be fined $100 if seen in public without a smile on their face. Exemptions include time spent visiting patients in hospitals or attending funerals.

Dear Mabel,
Please wear these at all times!
Only take them out for cleaning!
Your loving Husband xx

564 Vermont: Women must obtain written permission from their husbands to wear false teeth.

565 Asheville, North Carolina: It is illegal to sneeze on city streets.

566 Oklahoma: People who make ugly faces at dogs may be fined and jailed.

Hello POLICE!
I'm a small white dog in trouble!
Please send the DOG SQUAD around. I've got a man pulling faces at me who needs to go to jail!

567 Arkansas: A man is allowed to beat his wife, but no more than once a month.

568 Chicago, Illinois: It is illegal for a woman who weighs more than 200 lb (91 kg) to ride a horse while wearing shorts.

569 San Francisco: It is illegal to use old underwear to clean cars in a car wash.

570 A few years ago, a city council member in Albuquerque tried to have Santa Claus banned from the city. He failed.

571 San Francisco: There is a ban on any mechanical device that reproduces obscene language.

572 **A**ncient Egypt: The penalty for killing a cat, even by accident, was death.

573 **N**ew York: It is illegal to have a puppet show in your window.

574 **S**an Francisco: Sneezing powders and stink balls are prohibited.

The laws of New York might say a dog can't sleep in a bath... but it doesn't say you can't bath a dog in one!

Could someone pass me the plastic submarine and rubber duckie?

575 **N**ew York: It is illegal to let your dog sleep in the bathtub.

576 **M**esquite, Texas: Young people are not allowed to have haircuts that are "startling or unusual."

Wow Ray-mond! That looks great! Where did you learn to use those shears like that?

I learnt that shearing sheep! I only quit that job a couple of weeks back.

Unable to find a hairdresser in Texas who was willing to break the law to give him an 'unusual haircut'... Dennis slipped across the border into Oklahoma to go to his favourite salon.

577 **F**airbanks, Alaska: It is illegal to give a moose a beer.

578 **W**ashington State: Fake wrestling is not permitted.

KILLER and KARLA KOX the family wrestling team leave the casualty ward after a wrestling match in Seattle.

579 **T**urkey: In the sixteenth and seventeenth centuries, anyone caught drinking coffee was put to death.

580 **R**ussia: During the time of Peter the Great, any man who wore a beard had to pay a special tax.

581 **F**lorida: It is illegal to doze off under a hairdryer.

582 **G**eorgia: It is illegal to slap an old friend on the back.

Sgt. Smith kept mentioning it being illegal to nod off under a drier as Delores fought back sleep at the hairdressers.

583 **M**issouri: It is illegal to play hopscotch on a Sunday.

584 **B**oston: In the nineteenth century, it was illegal to bathe without a doctor's prescription.

585 **C**onnecticut: It is illegal to walk across the street on your hands.

586 **A**vignon, France: It is illegal for a flying saucer to land in the city.

A scene in the night sky over Avignon, France, where it's illegal for flying saucers to land....

You must understand. You cannot land here in our city of Avignon, you dirty space dogs!

Go land in Paris instead.'

AVIGNON

587 **N**orth Carolina: It is illegal to sell cotton lint or cotton seed at night.

588 **S**witzerland: It was once against the law to slam your car door.

Gunther loses the very same door his wife slammed in an argument only ten minutes before in the fast lane of the motorway at 60 mph.

589 **A**thens, Greece: A driver's license can be taken away if the driver is deemed either unbathed or poorly dressed.

590 **H**artford, Connecticut: It is illegal to plant a tree in the street.

Veronica left for work to find the "Set The Trees Free" organization had set two trees free illegally in her street.

591 **M**assachusetts: An old ordinance requires a person to have a permit to grow a goatee.

592 **F**lorida: Housewives are not allowed to break more than three dishes a day.

593 **P**araguay: Duelling is legal as long as both people are registered blood donors.

594 **C**hristiansburg, Virginia: It is illegal to spit.

595 **P**rovincetown, Massachusetts: It is illegal to sell suntan oil before noon on a Sunday.

596 **L**ouisiana: Biting someone with your natural teeth is assault, while biting someone with your false teeth is aggravated assault.

597 **S**an Francisco: It is illegal to beat a rug in front of your house.

598 **A**twoodville, Connecticut: People cannot play Scrabble while waiting for a politician to speak.

599 **N**ew York: It is illegal to do anything against the law.

History Never Repeats

600 The carnival made its debut in North America in 1894.

601 The parachute was invented by Leonardo da Vinci in 1515.

602 Cleopatra was Greek, not Egyptian.

603 In 1867, the Russian Czar Alexander II sold Alaska for about $7.2 million to the USA to pay off his gambling debts. At the time, most people thought this was a really bad deal for the USA.

Mamma mia!

If-a I surviva this-a fall I'm-a gonna call-a this a parachute!

Leonardo Da Vinci invents the parachute by accident by taking a fall from his villa roof while hanging out washing.

604 In the Middle Ages, pepper was used for bartering, and it was often more valuable than gold.

605 The oldest restaurant still in business opened in China in 1153.

606 Early bagpipes were made from the livers of sheep.

607 In 1859 in Glamorgan, Wales, a shower of fish fell from the sky.

608 Napoleon constructed his battle plans in a sandbox.

Napoleon plans the Battle of Waterloo in a sandbox.

609 Hawaii officially joined the USA on June 14 1900.

610 **I**n nineteenth-century Britain, you could be hanged for writing graffiti on Westminster Bridge.

611 **A**thletes in the ancient Olympics competed in the nude.

612 **M**oney made out of leather was once used in Russia.

613 **T**he Japanese throne has been occupied by a member of the same family since the sixth century. The present emperor is the 125th in succession.

614 **T**he umbrella originated in ancient Egypt, where it was used by the royal family and nobles as a symbol of rank.

615 The first vending machine was invented in 215 BC and was a water dispenser.

616 The Roman Empire existed from about 700 BC, when legend has it that Romulus and Remus founded Rome, to 1453, when the Eastern, or Byzantine, branch of the Empire fell to the Turks.

617 The Vikings reached North America 500 years before the Pilgrims.

618 The Tower of London is currently the home of the British crown jewels. It has been a zoo, an observatory, a mint, and a prison.

619 The first product made by Sony was a rice cooker.

620 The dinosaurs were on Earth for almost 150 million years. That is 75 times longer than humans have been on the planet.

621 Napoleon Bonaparte designed the Italian flag.

622 Before 1800, separate shoes for right and left feet were not designed.

623 The cigarette lighter was invented before the match.

624 Britain's youngest prime minister was William Pitt in 1783. He was 24 years old.

625 Tea is believed to have been discovered in 2737 BC by a Chinese emperor when some tea leaves accidentally blew into a pot of boiling water.

626 Thomas Sullivan of New York invented the tea bag in 1908.

627 Henry III became king when he was ten months old.

628 Air-filled tires were used on bicycles before they were used on cars.

629 King George I of England could not speak English.

630 Mexico once had three different presidents in 24 hours.

631 The first email was sent in 1972.

632 A squirrel closed down the New York stock exchange one day in 1987 when it burrowed through a phone line.

633 In ancient Egypt, certain baboons were mummified when they died.

634 The American army tried to train bats to drop bombs during World War II.

635 Sunglasses were invented by the Chinese in the thirteenth century.

636 In 1894, there were only four cars in the USA.

637 Denmark has the oldest existing national flag. The flag dates back to the thirteenth century.

The world's oldest existing flag from Denmark is hoisted in a strong breeze for the first time since the thirteenth century.

638 The oldest toy in the world is the doll. It was invented in Greece about 3000 years ago.

How silly! In the Middle Ages they believed the center of human intelligence was in the heart! Everyone knows it's in your big toe! Woh! Don't squeeze those brains too hard!

639 It was widely believed in the Middle Ages that the heart was the center of human intelligence.

640 Big Ben, a clock in London, once lost time when a group of birds used the minute hand as a perch.

641 Before 1600, New Year's Day was in March.

642 According to Aristotle, the brain's primary purpose was to cool the blood.

643 In the tenth century, the Grand Vizier of Persia carried his library on 400 trained camels. The camels had to walk in alphabetical order.

644 In ancient Egypt, men and women wore eyeshadow made from crushed beetles.

645 In ancient Japan, public contests were held to see who could fart the loudest and longest.

646 Chrysler built the B-29s that bombed Japan. Mitsubishi built the Zeros that tried to shoot the B-29s down. Both companies now build cars in a joint plant called Diamond Star.

647 The story of Cinderella originated in China.

648 In the nineteenth century, the British navy attempted to disprove the superstition that Friday is an unlucky day to embark on a ship. The keel of a new ship was laid on a Friday, the ship was named HMS *Friday*, she was commanded by a Captain Friday, and she finally went to sea on a Friday. The ship and her crew were never heard of again.

649 In ancient Egypt, monkeys were trained to pick fruit for harvest.

650 The most popular game ever for coin-operated machines is Pac-Man.

651 The formula for cold cream has hardly changed in the 1700 years since it was created by the Roman physician Galen.

652 Queen Elizabeth II of England sent her first email in 1976.

Queen Elizabeth sends her first email...then learns how to surf the internet for great car sites shortly after.

653 Coca-Cola was originally green.

654 Leonardo da Vinci invented scissors.

Leonardo Da Vinci quickly invents the scissors to get him out of one of his other inventions... ...the parachute.

655 The first television commercial was broadcast in 1941. It cost $9 to air.

The first TV commercial cost only $9 to air.

656 The oldest existing governing body, the Althing, operates in Iceland. It was established in AD 930.

657 People started keeping ferrets as pets 500 years before cats were kept as pets.

658 The largest coins were made from copper and were about 3 ft (1 m) long and 2 ft (60 cm) wide. They were used in Alaska in the nineteenth century and were worth $2500.

Wilbur struggles to the store with a huge Alaskan coin.

659 **D**emocracy began 2500 years ago in Athens, Greece.

660 **T**he Sumerians, who lived in the Middle East, invented the wheel in about 3450 BC.

661 **L**eonardo da Vinci invented an alarm clock that woke you by tickling your feet.

Leonardo Da Vinci is woken by the alarm clock he invented.

662 **W**hen tea was first introduced in the American colonies, many people did not know how to drink it. They served the tea leaves with sugar or syrup and threw away the water the leaves had been boiled in.

663 The wheelbarrow was invented in ancient China.

664 Long ago, thermometers were filled with brandy instead of mercury.

665 The first toy balloon, made of vulcanized rubber, was invented in London in 1847.

666 The Olympic torch and flame were invented by Germany for the 1936 Berlin Olympics.

667 Illegal gambling houses in eighteenth-century England employed a person to swallow the dice if there was a police raid.

668 The first message sent over Alexander Graham Bell's telephone on March 10 1876 was: "Mr. Watson, come here, I want you."

669 The Romans were famous for their amazing feasts. They loved to eat exotic foods like snails, swans, crows, horses, and peacocks.

670 In the Philippines during the 1500s, the yo-yo was made of stone and used as a weapon.

671 Ancient Egyptians slept on pillows made of stone.

672 Bread was used as an eraser before rubber erasers were invented.

673 **I**n nineteenth-century Britain, you could be hanged for being on a highway with a sooty face.

674 **S**ince its discovery in 1930, Pluto has completed only about 20 percent of its orbit. The last time Pluto was in its present position was before the American Revolution.

675 **M**ailing an entire building has been illegal in the USA since 1916 when a man mailed a brick house across Utah to avoid high freight rates.

676 **N**apoleon Bonaparte was afraid of cats.

The Battle of Waterloo is called off when Napoleon catches sight of a large ginger tom strolling across the battlefield.

677 Tomato sauce was sold in the 1830s as medicine.

678 In *Gulliver's Travels,* Jonathan Swift described the two moons of Mars, giving their exact sizes and speeds of rotation. He did this more than 100 years before the moons were discovered.

679 Long ago, clans that wanted to get rid of unpopular people would burn their houses down, hence the expression "to get fired."

680 The word "checkmate" in chess comes from the Persian phrase "Shah Mat", which means "the king is dead."

681 **D**entists in medieval Japan extracted teeth by pulling them out with their fingers.

682 **H**itler was *Time* magazine's Man of the Year in 1938.

683 **C**leopatra sometimes wore a fake beard.

Hatshepsut my faithful hand maiden. What do you think about this fake beard?

It looks just great with that Egyptian cotton dress and big hat your Majesty! Maybe just add some high heels?

684 **P**rior to World War II, when guards were posted at the fence, anyone could walk up to the front door of the American president's residence, the White House.

685 **E**arly Greeks and Romans used dried watermelons for helmets.

The early Greeks and Romans experimented with a variety of fruit and vegetables before settling on watermelons for helmets.

Oh Maximus... You're always so theatrical!

686 The world's first speed limit was introduced in England in 1903. It was 20 miles (32 km) per hour.

687 The first daily television broadcast began in 1936 on the BBC.

688 In nineteenth-century Britain, you could be hanged for stealing a spoon.

689 Karate originated in India, but was developed further in China.

Weird World Facts

690 The state of Florida is larger than England.

691 The Earth spins at 1000 miles (1600 km) per hour at the equator.

Hey... What are you doing?

HANGING ON! I've just found out the Earth is spinning at 1000 miles per hour!

692 A lump of pure gold the size of a matchbox can be flattened into a sheet of gold the size of a tennis court.

693 **M**eteorites slam into the Earth every year.

694 **T**he Earth rotates more slowly on its axis in March than in September.

695 **E**urope is the only continent without a desert.

696 **T**he Pacific Ocean is not as salty as the Atlantic Ocean.

697 **D**iamonds are flammable.

698 **I**t would take a bullet fired from Earth more than 20 years to reach the Sun.

699 **I**n Japan, there are vending machines for underwear.

700 In 1980, there was a traffic jam in France that was 109 miles (176 km) long.

701 The Earth flies through space at more than 66 600 miles (100 000 km) per hour.

702 Candles burn better when they are frozen.

703 The largest continent is Asia.

704 Micro-organisms can be found as deep as 2 miles (3.5 km) in the Earth's crust.

705 The South Pole is colder than the North Pole.

706 The USA creates nearly 20 percent of the world's garbage.

707 The first living creature to orbit the Earth was a dog sent into space by the Russians.

708 All international pilots, no matter where they are from, are required to speak English.

709 In a study by the University of Chicago in 1907, it was found that yellow is the easiest color to spot.

710 There are more chickens in the world than people.

711 The Greek national anthem has 158 verses.

712 In the Amazon rainforest, 1 sq mile (2.5 sq km) can be home to 3000 species of trees.

713 The moon moves 1.5 in (3.82 cm) away from the Earth every year.

714 Bishop's Rock in the UK is the smallest island in the world.

715 A third of our water gets flushed down the toilet.

716 Damascus in Syria is the oldest inhabited city. It was founded in 753 BC.

717 Australia is the only country that takes up an entire continent.

718 The British flag should only be called the Union Jack when it is on a ship at sea.

719 California, USA, has the fifth largest economy in the world.

720 More than half of the USA coastline is in Alaska.

721 A storm officially becomes a hurricane when it reaches wind speeds of 74 miles (119 km) per hour.

722 In Bangladesh, school children can be jailed for cheating on their exams.

723 **H**alf the world's population is under 25 years old.

724 **T**here are about 1800 thunderstorms occurring on Earth at any given time.

725 **T**he deepest part of the Pacific Ocean is 6.8 miles (11 km).

726 **I**n Australia and the UK, light switches are flicked down for on. In the USA, the switch is flicked up for on.

727 **E**very year in Sweden, a hotel is built out of ice. It melts, then it is rebuilt the next year.

728 Almost half the people on Earth have never made a phone call.

729 There are more than 50 000 earthquakes throughout the world every year.

730 The center of the Earth is believed to be as hot as the surface of the Sun.

731 The most abundant metal in the ground is aluminium.

732 Icebergs have been fitted with sailing gear and sailed 2400 miles (3840 km).

733 The amount of water on Earth is the same now as when the planet formed 4.54 billion years ago.

734 **B**igger raindrops make brighter rainbows.

735 **P**roportionally speaking, the Earth is smoother than a billiard ball.

736 **D**isney World in Florida is twice the size of Manhattan Island.

The Earth was supposed to be as smooth as a billiard ball... But Bob hit a rough patch over North America that sent his 9 ball right off the table.

737 **I**t takes one drop of ocean water more than 1000 years to circulate around the world.

738 **T**he Earth is slightly hotter during a full moon.

Feeling hotter tonight, Claude?

No. Why? Am I supposed to? The tin roof's a little warm!

Well the Earth is supposed to be warmer during a full moon so they say!

739 **R**ussia and America are less than 2.5 miles (4 km) apart at their closest point.

740 There are solar-powered pay phones in the Saudi Arabian desert.

741 An estimated 95 percent of all forms of life that once existed on Earth are now extinct.

742 The international dialling code for Antarctica is 67.

743 Waves in the Pacific Ocean can be up to 111 ft (34 m) high.

744 The Earth is 80 times the size of the moon.

745 It takes eight minutes and 17 seconds for light from the Sun to reach Earth.

746 February 1865 is the only month in recorded history that did not have a full moon.

747 The Amazon River pushes lots of water into the Atlantic Ocean. In fact, there is fresh water in the ocean more than 100 miles (160 km) from the mouth of the river.

748 Eighty percent of people who are hit by lightning are men.

749 The average meteor is no larger than a grain of sand, but it is moving at nearly 30 000 miles (48 000 km) per hour when it enters the atmosphere. This makes it burn so brightly that it is seen as a "shooting star" from the ground.

750 **A** raindrop falls at about 7.5 miles (12 km) per hour.

751 **D**uring a severe storm, the Empire State Building may sway slightly to either side.

Food for Thought

752 Fine-grained volcanic ash is an ingredient in some toothpastes.

753 A person would have to drink more than 12 cups of hot cocoa to consume the amount of caffeine found in one cup of coffee.

754 A favorite dish in old England was lark's tongue.

755 In Vietnam, there is a drink made from lizard blood.

Little Rupert couldn't bear to see his Mom cry while cutting onions. So spitting his gum on the floor did the trick. She couldn't cut the onions.

I was about to start cutting these onions...and now I've trod in this awful chewing gum.

756 **C**hewing gum can keep a person from crying while cutting onions.

757 **B**lack pepper is the most popular spice in the world.

758 **A** Tanzanian dish is white ant pie.

759 **W**orld-eating record #1 is 12 slugs in two minutes.

Tanzanian white ant pie should always be eaten straight away. And never ever left out on a wooden table to cool.

As hard as Walter tried, he just couldn't get that 13th slimy slug down to beat his previous World Record of 12 slugs in two minutes.

Just one more little slug!

WORLD SLUG EATING CONTEST

760 **E**ggs are sold on bits of string in Korea.

761 **A** favorite dish of Indian princes was a sparrow stuffed inside a quail stuffed inside a sand grouse stuffed inside a chicken stuffed inside a peacock stuffed inside a goat stuffed inside a camel and roasted underground until it was tender.

762 **S**ome Amazonian tribes like to barbecue tarantulas and eat them. Apparently, they taste like prawns.

How the Jaguar tribe from the Amazon relax around the barbecue.

763 **B**anana plants cannot reproduce themselves. They must be propagated by people.

764 **W**orld-eating record #2 is 28 cockroaches in four minutes.

765 **U**nless you have a doctor's note, it is illegal to buy ice cream after 6 p.m. in Newark, New Jersey.

766 **N**achos is the food most often craved by pregnant women.

767 **R**at meat sausages were once a delicacy in the Philippines.

768 **C**anned food was invented in 1813, but a practical can opener was not invented until 1870.

769 **B**ecause Hindus do not eat beef, McDonald's in New Delhi makes lamb hamburgers.

770 **T**he blue whale needs to consume 1.5 million calories a day.

771 **G**enghis Khan killed his brother after an argument over a fish.

772 **W**orld-eating record #3 is 60 worms in three minutes.

773 **P**eanuts are one of the ingredients in dynamite.

774 **W**omen swallow and digest most of the lipstick they apply.

775 **R**ubber bands last longer when refrigerated.

776 **A** Japanese dish is broiled beetle grubs.

777 **W**orld-eating record #4 is 13 raw eggs in two seconds.

778 The annual harvest of an entire coffee tree makes 1 lb (450 g) of ground coffee.

779 Koalas do not drink water.

780 The first Harley Davidson motorcycle built in 1903 used a tomato can for a carburettor.

781 Bubble gum contains rubber.

782 A cure for whooping cough in old Ireland was sheep's droppings boiled in milk.

783 **A** popular dish in Belize contains mashed and roasted cockroaches.

784 **W**orld-eating record #5 is 144 snails in 11 minutes.

785 **A** favorite meal in China is sun-dried maggots.

786 **S**tannous fluoride, which is the cavity fighter found in toothpaste, is made from recycled tin.

787 **M**ost cows give more milk when they listen to music.

788 **M**ore people use blue toothbrushes than red ones.

789 Rain contains vitamin B12.

790 A Samoan dish is baked bat.

791 A favorite dish in Mexico is lamb brain tacos.

792 World-eating record #6 is 12 bananas with skins in four minutes.

793 In Ecuador, people used to eat boiled guinea pig.

794 The microwave was invented in the 1940s after a researcher walked by a radar tube and discovered that a chocolate bar in his pocket had melted.

795 Until the sixteenth century, carrots were black, green, red, and purple. Then a Dutch horticulturist discovered some mutant yellow seeds that produced an orange color.

796 You are more likely to be killed by a champagne cork than by a venomous spider.

Despite a venomous spider being on the loose at the wedding... It was the bride's father with a champagne bottle they really had to fear.

797 Eating an apple will make you feel more awake in the morning than drinking a cup of coffee will.

798 Astronauts are not allowed to eat beans before they go into space because passing wind in a spacesuit damages it.

799 **M**ost lipsticks contain fish scales.

800 **A** favorite dish in Norway is beef blood pudding.

Erik from Norway tries out his
first beef blood pudding.

801 **W**orld-eating record #7 is 100 maggots in
five minutes.

Wacky Word Facts

802 **N**o words in the English language rhyme with month, orange, silver, or purple.

803 **"G**o" is the shortest sentence in the English language.

804 **T**he word "paradise" was once the Persian word for a royal amusement park.

805 **T**he Cambodian alphabet is the largest. It has 74 letters.

806 The Hawaiian alphabet consists of only 12 letters.

807 The longest word in English is "pneumonoultramicroscopicsilicovolcanoconiosis."

808 Aardvark means "earth pig."

809 The only 15-letter word that can be spelled without repeating a letter is "uncopyrightable."

810 The name "jeep" comes from the abbreviation used in the army for the general purpose vehicle, GP.

811 The Inuit (Eskimos) have 20 different words for snow.

812 Dr. Seuss invented the word "nerd."

813 The computer term "bug" originated in the days when computers were made from vacuum tubes. Bugs liked to live in the warm tubes and this sometimes caused short circuits.

814 "Zorro" is Spanish for "fox."

The great Mexican super hero...Zorro (the fox)

815 The word "news" is actually an acronym for the four compass points (north, east, west, and south).

816 Attics were invented in Attica.

817 The first word spoken on the moon was "Okay."

When I told him the Lunar Module was out of fuel and we couldn't bring him back to Earth...You know what he said? ...OKAY!

He said OKAY?

He must have left his hearing aid batteries at home on his dressing table!

818 The oldest word in the English language is "town."

819 The word "diastima" means having a gap between your teeth.

820 The gorilla's scientific name is *Gorilla gorilla*.

821 The longest one-syllable word in the English language is "screeched."

822 More people in China speak English than in the USA.

823 The word "Mrs." cannot be written in full.

824 The dot over the letter "i" is called the tittle.

825 Butterflies used to be called "flutterbys."

826 "Aloha" means both "goodbye" and "hello" in Hawaiian.

827 The "sixth sick sheik's sixth sheep's sick" is the toughest tongue-twister in the English language.

828 **A** "spat" is a baby oyster.

829 **T**he word "queueing" is the only English word with five consecutive vowels.

830 **N**ewton is the most common place name in Britain. There are 150 places with that name.

831 **I**n England in the 1880s, "pants" was considered a dirty word.

832 **"D**reamt" is the only English word that ends in the letters "mt."

833 **"O**f" is the only word in which an "f" is pronounced like a "v."

Ebineezer's wife took advantage of the London sales of Christmas 1882.
She snapped up as much cheap imported curtain material as she could find.
By turning it into pants for her husband, she gave not only him a bad name ...but PANTS a bad name as well...

834 **A** pregnant goldfish is called a twit.

835 "Bookkeeper" and "bookkeeping" are the only words in the English language with three consecutive sets of double letters.

836 The word "taxi" is spelled the same in English, German, French, Swedish, and Portuguese.

837 The most used letter in the English alphabet is "e", and "q" is the least used.

838 The word "karaoke" means "empty orchestra."

839 The sentence "the quick brown fox jumps over the lazy dog" uses every letter in the alphabet.

Strange Science

840 **G**lass is made from sand.

Come and make sandcastles Edward!

Come in, for a swim Eddie!

Now... I'll just calculate how many glass bottles could be made out of all of the sand on every beach in the world!

841 **G**lass, which looks like a solid, is actually a very slow-moving liquid.

While the other kids took their buckets and spades to the beach...Edward the nerd took his calculator.

842 **A**n iceberg contains more heat than a lighted match.

Well...If an iceberg contains more heat than a lighted match...I guess that eventually that heat is going to melt that iceberg!

843 **V**elcro was invented by a person who studied the burrs that clung to his dog's coat after a walk.

844 White light is a mixture of all the colors in the spectrum.

845 Eleanor Roosevelt received a telegram from the 1939 World's Fair in New York that used only the power from electric eels.

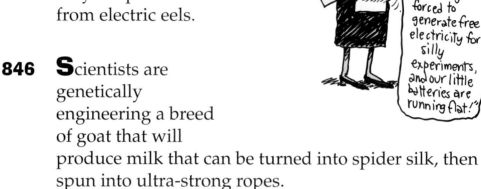

846 Scientists are genetically engineering a breed of goat that will produce milk that can be turned into spider silk, then spun into ultra-strong ropes.

847 Some forms of primitive life can survive anywhere that water is found, even in boiling water or ice.

848 The sound of a whip cracking is actually a mini sonic boom that occurs when the tip of the whip breaks the sound barrier.

849 Using nanotechnology, a microscopic guitar with strings has been made. It is no larger than a blood cell.

850 The temperature on the moon can drop by up to 500°F (260°C) at night.

851 During one four-year period, inventor Thomas Edison registered almost 300 patents.

852 John Logie Baird made the first television in 1924 using cardboard, scrap wood, needles, string, and other materials.

853 More than 1000 new insects are discovered every year.

854 In 1889, the commissioner of the United States Patent Office announced that "Everything that can be invented, has been invented."

855 Toilet paper was invented in New York in 1857.

856 The first video-cassette recorder was built in 1956. It was the size of an upright piano.

857 A cross between a goat and a sheep is called a "geep."

858 Thomas Edison was afraid of the dark.

Maybe Thomas Edison invented the light bulb because he was afraid of the dark.

859 The computer term "byte" is short for "by eight."

860 Arecibo observatory in Puerto Rico has one of the largest radio telescopes in the world. It is over 1000 ft (300 m) across and could pick up the signal from a cell phone on Jupiter.

Let's see just how well that Arecibo radio telescope works down there on Earth. I'm going to order a pizza to be delivered on this cell phone from a store in Puerto Rico.

861 English chemist John Walker never patented his invention of matches because he felt such an important tool should be public property.

862 Florence Nightingale did not believe in bacteria.

863 Sir Isaac Newton invented the cat flap.

Oh Kitty! My poor little Kitty! Just like why an apple falls from a tree ...I have a theory for why you hit that door and bounced off! You need a catflap in the door that opens my friend!

864 The world's smallest motor was built at the Berkeley campus of the University of California. Three hundred of the motors could line up on the stump left when you cut a hair.

865 Honey is sometimes used in antifreeze mixtures and in the center of golf balls.

866 The Eiffel Tower always leans away from the Sun because heat makes the metal expand.

867 You can start a fire by using a lens-shaped piece of ice and concentrating a beam of sunlight onto flammable material.

868 The electric chair was invented by a dentist.

I thought to myself...there's something about this dentist that gives me the creeps. Perhaps it was the look on his face. ...The hard uncomfortable wooden seat... the belts that tightened around me ... or the talk of exceptionally large power bills.. or was it unusual that a dentist should talk about inventing ...THE ELECTRIC CHAIR!

869 The first stethoscope was made in 1816 with a roll of paper.

I can't hear a heartbeat my good fellow! All I can hear is a sound like a paper tube crumbling!

CRUNCH

I think you're in trouble

Me too!

870 Cat urine glows under a black light.

871 Hot water freezes more quickly than cold water.

Patent Mania

872 Patent no. GB2272154 is for a ladder to enable spiders to climb out of a bath. The ladder comprises a thin, flexible strip of latex rubber that follows the inner contours of the bath. A suction pad on the ladder is attached to the top of the bath.

873 Patent no. GB2060081 is for a horse-powered minibus. The horse walks along a conveyor belt in the middle of the bus. This drives the wheels via a gearbox. A thermometer under the horse's collar is connected to the vehicle instrument panel. The driver can signal to the horse using a handle, which brings a mop into contact with the horse.

874 Patent no. GB2172200 is for an umbrella for wearing on the head. The support frame is designed not to mess up the wearer's hair.

875 Patent no. GB2289222 is for a fart-collecting device. It comprises a gas-tight collecting tube for insertion into the rectum of the subject. The tube is connected to a gas-tight collecting bag. The end of the tube inserted into the subject is covered with a gauze filter and a gas permeable bladder.

876 Patent no. US6325727 is for an underwater golf swing training device. The device has a hydrodynamically adjustable paddle that can be altered manually. This provides variable resistance to the user as he or she swings the device through the water.

Bob, trying out his new underwater golf swing training device, tries for the bunker but only manages the side of the smimming pool.

877 Patent no. GB2267208 is for a portable seat that is worn on a waist-belt. The seat cushion can pivot from a stowed position to a seating position.

878 Patent no. US4233942 is for a device for protecting the ears of a long-haired dog from becoming soiled by food while it is eating. A tube contains each of the dog's ears. The tubes are held away from the dog's mouth and food while it eats.

879 Patent no. WO9701384 is for a leash for walking an imaginary pet. It has a preformed shape and supports a simulated pet harness and collar. A micro loudspeaker in the collar is connected to an integrated circuit in the handle, to produce a variety of barks and growls.

880 Patent no. GB1453920 is for rolled-up fire curtains at roof level on a skyscraper. When a fire starts, the curtains are released to cover the building and suffocate the fire.

Rusty tried the TURBO TUTTI-FRUITY on the low setting...but wasn't getting enough tutti-fruity. So he gave it a go ...on high.

881 Patent no. US5971829 is for a motorized ice-cream cone. The cone spins while you lick the ice cream.

882 Patent no. US2760763 is for an egg beater that beats the egg within its shell.

Boy! It's cooler in this shade! But the heat must be getting to me! Where did I put my drink?

883 Patent no. US6637447 is for the "Beerbrella." This is a tiny umbrella that clips onto a beer bottle, keeping the sun off the beverage.

884 Patent no. WO98/21939 is for deer ears. To use, simply place the deer ears on your head and swivel your new ears in the direction you would like to hear.

885 Patent no. US3150831 is for a birthday cake candle extinguisher.

886 Patent no. US5713081 is for three-legged pantihose. When there is a run in the stocking, you simply rotate your leg into the spare hose. The damaged hose is then tucked into a pocket in the crotch of the pantihose.

887 Patent no. US5719656 is for earless eyewear. Stick the self-adhesive magnets on to each side of your head. The eyewear frames contain internal magnets that hold on to the magnets on your temples.

888 Patent no. US4022227 is for a three way comb-over to cover a bald head. Just let your hair grow long at the sides, then divide it into three sections, and comb it over your bald head one section at a time.

889 Patent no. US4344424 is for a mouth cage that is designed to allow you to breathe and speak but not eat.

890 Patent no. US4872422 is for a pet petter. This is an electronic device consisting of an eye that spots your pet and signals the electronic motors to activate the petting arm. The arm is tipped with a human-like hand for added realism.

891 Patent no. USD342712 is for a frame that clamps around your pet's waist and supports a clear plastic tent-like structure that keeps your pet dry in the rain. There are air holes in the tent.

892 Patent no. US6557994 is for a way to hang eyeglasses on your face. You use body piercing studs. Pierce your eyebrows and hang your glasses from the studs. There is also a design that works with a nose bridge stud.

893 Patent no. US6266930 is for a "Squabble Shield." The shield is a shatterproof, clear plexiglass wall that fits in the middle of the back seat of a family car. It keeps children apart, and from squabbling, while the parent is driving.

894 Patent no. US4825469 is for a fully inflatable motorcycle suit. When the rider falls off the bike, the suit swells with compressed gas until it covers the head, arms, torso, and legs, protecting the rider from damage.

895 Patent no. US4365889 is for a wristband with an absorbent pad. People with colds can wipe their noses on it. It also has a cover that flips down, keeping all the nasties inside.

896 Patent no. US4299921 is for the "Smell This" breath mask. You check if your breath is smelly by placing the mask on your face, then breathing out through your mouth, and breathing in through your nose.

897 Patent no. US3842343 is for mud flaps to keep mud from flying up the back of your shoes.

898 Patent no. US6704666 is for the "Speak & Swing," which is a motorized golf club selection system. You simply speak to your golf bag, telling it which club you want, and the club automatically pops up.

899 Patent no. US5372954 is for the "Wig Flipper." A wig is placed on a large spring and attached to a small cap. The wig and spring are then compressed, locked onto the cap, and placed on your head. When you push the spring release button, the hairpiece will jump into the air.

900 Patent no. US6600372 is for the "Spitting Duck." This device fits most toilets and, instead of using toilet paper, you lift the duck's bill, and a strategically placed nozzle will spray your bottom with the cleaning formula.

901 Patent US5352633 is for the "Arm Mitten," which the driver of a car wears on one arm. This protects the arm from sunburn when the elbow rests on the window ledge.

902 Patent no. US6630345 is for the "Wonder Butt Bra," which lifts, supports, and shapes a person's butt, giving it a desirable shape. It is fully adjustable to fit all sizes of butts.

903 Patent no. US5848443 is for the "Travel Relief." This is a padded toilet for use while driving. It even flushes.

904 Patent US5375340 is for "Cool Shoes," which are air-conditioned shoes that have a mini-network of heat exchange coils built into the heels. With each step, the wearer activates the compressor chamber, which forces cool air up into the shoe via a rubber bladder in the sole.

905 Patent US5130161 is for the "Life Expectancy Watch." You program the watch by answering questions about your lifestyle. Your estimated remaining time on Earth is displayed in years, months, days, and hours.

Hilarious Humans

906 Every person has a unique tongue print.

907 Your right lung takes in more air than your left lung does.

908 A woman's heart beats faster than a man's.

909 The inventor of Vaseline ate a spoonful of the stuff every morning.

910 Albert Einstein never wore socks.

Albert Einstein never wore socks...because he always wore Bermuda shorts and thongs. And socks look awful with thongs!

911 **A**stronauts get taller when they are in space.

912 **P**eople photo-copying their butts is the cause of 23 percent of all photocopier malfunctions.

913 **I**t is impossible to cry in space because of the lack of gravity.

914 **B**ill Gates's house was designed using a Macintosh computer.

915 **O**nly one percent of bacteria are harmful to humans.

916 **Y**our eyes use 25 percent of your brain power.

917 In Brazil in 1946, a woman gave birth to decaplets (ten children). She had eight girls and two boys.

918 To be a NASA astronaut your height cannot exceed 6 ft (182 cm).

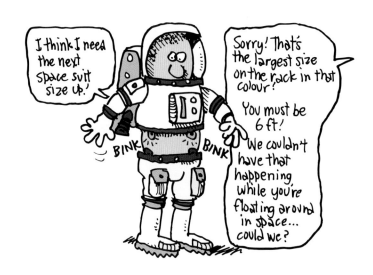

919 There are four basic tastes the human tongue can detect. Salty and sweet are tasted on the tip of the tongue, bitter is tasted at the base of the tongue, and sour is tasted along the sides of the tongue.

920 The average person blinks about 24 times per minute or about 12.5 million times per year.

921 **W**edding rings are worn on the fourth finger of the left hand because people used to believe that the vein in this finger goes directly to the heart.

922 **T**he average human dream lasts two to three seconds.

923 **T**wenty-five percent of your bones are located in your feet.

If twenty-five percent of your bones are located in your feet... that means I've just broken a quarter of the bones in my body!

924 **A**lbert Einstein's eyes were auctioned in 1994 after being stored in a safety deposit box since his death in 1955.

Next in today's auction we have ITEM Nº 425 Listed as ~ "TWO LOVELY EYES IN A JAR!"

Ummm ... Geeeee.... Right-o.... Believed to have belonged to Mr Albert Einstein.

So... for any of you who are collectors of Mr Einstein's body parts... Do we have a first bid please?

AUCTION

925 **T**he numbers of births in India each year exceeds the entire population of Australia (22 million).

926 The world's human population was only five million in 5000 BC.

927 If the population of China lined up and you had to walk the length of the line, you would be walking forever because of all the new births.

928 Every year 4000 people injure themselves with teapots.

929 The measurement from your wrist to your elbow is the same measurement as your foot.

930 Nearly 10 percent of American households dress their pets in Halloween costumes.

931 **A**rteries carry blood away from the heart. Veins carry blood toward the heart.

932 **A**ccording to a study by the Economic Research Service, 27 percent of all food produced in Western nations ends up in garbage bins. Yet 1.2 billion people in the world are underfed.

933 **G**irls have more taste buds than boys do.

934 **T**here are only 200 family names in China for a population of well over a billion.

935 **Y**ou breathe in and out about 23 000 times a day.

936 The average height of people in Western nations has increased by 4 in (10 cm) in the last 150 years.

937 Roy Sullivan of Virginia, USA, was hit by lightning seven times.

938 One out of 20 people has an extra rib.

939 Douglas Bader was born in London in 1910. He flew for the Royal Air Force in World War II, but both his legs were amputated after his aeroplane crashed. He became a flight leader and was instrumental in the Battle of Britain. He attained 23 combat victories by the summer of 1941, making him the fifth highest scoring ace in the RAF.

940 New Zealand was the first country to give women the vote.

941 The average person has at least seven dreams a night.

942 A corpse left out in warm weather will be reduced to a skeleton in about nine days.

943 The most common name in the world is Mohammed.

944 In 1973, a confectionery salesman was buried in a coffin made of chocolate in accordance with his dying wishes.

945 Taste buds last about ten days. Of course, your body is making new ones all the time.

946 In India, people wear masks on the back of their heads when they go outside. This confuses tigers because they like to attack from the rear.

947 The Beijing Duck Restaurant in China can seat 9000 people.

948 Color blindness is ten times more common in men than in women.

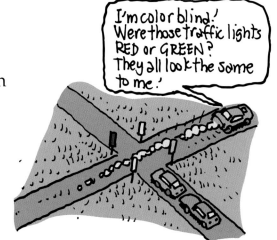

949 Humans spend a third of their lives sleeping.

950 **R**obots in Japan pay union dues.

951 **T**he Mbuti Pygmies are among the shortest people in the world. The average height for a man is 4 ft 6 in (137 cm) tall.

952 **L**ack of sleep will kill a person faster than starvation will.

953 **B**oanthropy is a disease that makes a person believe he or she is an ox.

954 **A** person cannot taste food unless it is mixed with saliva. For example, if salt is placed on a dry tongue, the taste buds will not be able to taste it. As soon as a drop of saliva is added and the salt is dissolved, the person tastes the salt.

955 Tibetans and Mongolians put salt in their tea instead of sugar.

956 Your tongue is the strongest muscle in your body.

957 Mosquitoes are more attracted to people who have recently eaten bananas.

958 Masai tribesman leave their dead out for wild animals to eat.

959 There are villages in Papua New Guinea that are only a 20-minute walk apart, but the villagers speak different languages.

960 The Neanderthal's brain was bigger than your brain is.

961 **A** pair of leather shoes can supply enough nourishment for a person for about a week.

962 **N**apoleon Bonaparte's penis was put up for auction in 1972. It did not sell. It was later purchased for $3800.

963 **T**he average person is 0.25 in (6.2 mm) taller at night.

964 **T**he Inuit (Eskimos) use fridges to stop their food from freezing.

965 **T**he only part of the human body that has no blood supply is the cornea of the eye. It takes in oxygen directly from the air.

966 Fingernails live for three to six months. They grow nearly 1.5 in (4 cm) a year.

967 A 4 in (10 cm) lock of Beethoven's hair sold at Sotheby's for £4000 in 1994.

968 Midgets and dwarfs usually have normal-size children.

969 In the USA, deaf people have safer driving records than people who can hear.

970 Forty percent of dog and cat owners carry pictures of their pets in their wallets.

971 Only 55 percent of Americans know that the sun is a star.

972 **H**uman skin sheds continually. The outer layer of skin is entirely replaced every 28 days.

973 **I**n 1980, a Las Vegas hospital suspended workers for betting on when patients would die.

974 **I**n Los Angeles, there are more cars than people.

975 **W**hen D. H. Lawrence died, his ashes were mixed with cement, then used to make his girlfriend's mantelpiece.

976 The body of Charlie Chaplin was stolen in 1978 from a Swiss graveyard and held for ransom. The sum demanded was 600 000 francs.

977 Even if up to 80 percent of it is removed, the human liver can continue to function and it will grow back to its original size.

978 Manhole covers are always round because they rest on a lip that is smaller than the cover. This means the cover cannot fit through the opening on any angle. A square or rectangular cover could fall through.

979 Your sense of smell is about five percent as strong as a dog's.

980 The pupil of a human eye will expand as much as 45 percent when it sees something pleasing.

981 Tibetans drink tea made with salt and rancid yak butter.

982 Even the cleverest person only uses one percent of the English language.

983 Men sweat 40 percent more than women do.

984 The greatest number of descendants belonged to Samuel Mast. When he died in 1992, at the age of 96, he had 824 living descendants.

985 The creator of the waffle iron did not like waffles.

986 Forty-two percent of people urinate in the shower.

987 The object that is most often choked on by Americans is the toothpick.

988 The average person laughs 15 times a day.

989 Chinese people make up more than 20 percent of the world's population.

990 The largest cell in the human body is the ovum, the female reproductive cell.

991 **D**uring your life, you will eat an average of 70 insects and ten spiders while sleeping.

Cecil leaves the bedroom window open and swallows most of his expected life's quota of 70 insects and ten spiders while he sleeps

992 **T**he longest beard on a woman was 11 in (27.9 cm).

993 **J**apanese speakers learn Spanish faster than they learn English. English speakers learn Spanish faster than they learn Japanese.

994 **T**he most productive mother gave birth to 69 children.

995 **I**n Albania, nodding your head means no and shaking it means yes.

Hello! I appear to be lost! Can you tell me please.. Is this the way to the AIRPORT?

OK! I realise you don't speak much English But you're nodding your head.. So you must mean...YES.

While asking an Albanian lady for directions Austin is unaware that in Albania people shake their heads for yes.. and nod for no. Austin ends up in neighbouring Serbia instead of the airport.

996 **W**hile you are reading this sentence, 50 000 cells in your body will have been replaced by new cells.

997 **A** baby excretes its own weight in faeces every 60 hours.

While sneezing can be known to break a rib... Sneezing while walking down stairs can be much more dangerous.

998 **A**lthough an extremely rare occurrence, sneezing too hard can fracture a rib.

999 **T**he average human body contains enough fat to make seven bars of soap.

Hey Barb! You're looking great! You've lost so much weight.

I know Cheryl. And I'd like you to have some of it.

Cheryl finds out that there's enough fat in the human body to make seven bars of soap.

1000 **B**abies are born without kneecaps. Kneecaps do not appear until a child is two years old.